Finding the Balance

A GUIDE TO SANE LIVING

Bonnie Barness

A Message from the Author

Dear Reader,

Many people go through life just getting by. They have a sense that something is missing, but they don't know what it is and look no further. You are different! You want more from life and are willing to search until you find it. This workbook will help you in that quest. By putting into practice the ideas expressed within these pages, you will begin to change your life forever.

Life is a journey. We can choose to be active participants or to just go along for the ride. It takes courage and determination to create the changes we long for. Believe in yourself, listen to your heart's desire and you will find the strength to go after your dreams.

My wish for you is that you achieve the balance and happiness you are striving for. Know that you are now about to take another important step on your personal road towards greater self-fulfillment. Be strong and honest, and you are sure to succeed.

Respectfully,

Bonnie Barnes

Table of Contents

Section	Activity	Page
A MESSAGE FROM THE AUTHOR		3
FEELING YOUR CENTER	Centered Moments	6
	Remember a Time	7
GETTING OUT OF BALANCE	The Process of Becoming Aware	10
FINDING THE BALANCE	Knowing Myself	14
	Making Centered Choices	15
	Stepping Out	16
Over-Extending	Over-Extended	18
	Prioritizing	19
	Re-Evaluating Commitments	20
Personal Fulfillment	Steps to Fulfillment	23
	The Pieces of My Life	24
	My Circle of Life	25
	Getting in Touch	27
	Making Room for New Dreams	28
Expectations	Expectation of Others	29
	Keeping My Power	31
	Is it Personal?	32
	Should I or Shouldn't I?	34
	Choosing My Actions	35
	Cognitive Techniques	38
	Taking Action	40
	Expectations of Myself	41
	Supporting Myself	42
Happiness is a Choice	Choosing Happiness	43
	Surviving Loss	44
STAYING IN BALANCE	My Well-Being, My Priority	46
	Journal Writing	47
	Protecting My Center	48
	Getting it On Paper	50
	Simplifying My Life	51
	Conflict Resolution	52
	Emotional Intelligence	54
	Problem-Solving	56
	On-Going Challenges	57
	Inner Growth	59
PERSONAL SUPPORT	Diagramming My Support	60
	Stress Management	61
	De-Stressing Techniques	62
	A Balanced Lifestyle	63
LIVING FROM YOUR CENTER	Connected to My True Self	66
ABOUT THE AUTHOR		67

Feeling Your Center

Centered Moments

In order to live in a balanced manner, we need to know what it feels like to be in balance. Think about times that you felt happy and fulfilled, when you had a sense of being centered and in control. Remember when you were in touch with your inner strength and saw its reflection in all that you did in the world.

In those moments you were feeling your Center, your True Authentic Self.

Living from your Center is about having these experiences all the time. We have the ability to create them no matter what is happening around us. The first key to being in balance is **Feeling Your Center.**

List times and circumstances when you have felt centered.

_____

_____

_____

List times and circumstances when your sense of well-being and inner strength was exceptionally strong.

_____

_____

_____

Remember a Time

Step One

Close your eyes.

Step Two

Remember a time when you felt centered and alive. Allow yourself to go back in time and connect with this amazing feeling.

Step Three

Stay with that feeling.

Step Four

Open you eyes.

Step Five

Write down a description or draw a picture which illustrates the feeling.

Step Six

Throughout your day, stop, close your eyes,
take a deep breath, and recapture that feeling.

Finding the Balance

Getting Out of Balance

The Process of Becoming Aware

How often do we begin our day feeling great and thinking that life is wonderful and then by the end of the day we are tired, depressed, and discouraged?
We ask ourselves, "What happened to all the joy and optimism of the morning?" Somehow through the course of the day it seemed to have gotten lost in the shuffle.

In order to live from our Center and feel balanced, we need to become aware of what causes us to get out of balance! The clearer we are of the causes, the greater is our ability to deal with them effectively. The first step in becoming more aware is to listen to the messages our body is sending us. Feeling tense, tired or irritable is our body's way of letting us know that we are getting out of balance.

The second step is to pay attention to our emotions. If we are feeling angry, sad, frustrated, or disappointed, we must take the time to stop what we are doing and look internally and externally for the cause. To look internally we must discover what we are thinking, and to look externally it is necessary to notice what is occurring around us.

Five common reasons that we get out of balance are:

1. We become over-extended.

2. We feel unfulfilled.

3. We let other people's behaviors significantly influence us.

4. We have unrealistic expectations of others and of ourselves.

5. We or those we are close to suffer a great loss.

The Process of Becoming Aware

List times and circumstances when you...

were over-extended

were negatively affected by other people's behavior

The Process of Becoming Aware

felt unfulfilled

were disappointed with others

were disappointed in yourself

were devastated because something terrible happened

Now, go back and write down next to each of your responses what you were experiencing physically and emotionally. Were you tired, tense, irritable, angry or sad?

Finding the Balance

Knowing Myself

To find the balance we are looking for it is necessary to know ourselves. We must be in touch with what we need to be happy. Often, we have chosen goals and taken on responsibilities without considering what effect they will have on our overall feeling of happiness. And then we wonder why we are not enjoying our lives as much as we think we should be. There are specific actions we can take to increase our sense of joy and expectancy. The first is being honest with ourselves concerning what our most important needs are and what our true limitations are. In order to gain more self-knowledge, we need to look into ourselves and ask these two questions.

What are my most important needs?

What are my limitations in terms of physical, mental and emotional energy?

Finding the Balance

Making Centered Choices

Every day we make decisions that affect the quality of our lives. It is important to make choices that take into consideration what we need to be happy and to feel in balance. Next time you have a decision to make, ask yourself:

What decisions am I making right now in my life?

What options am I considering?

Which choices will support my staying in balance?

Which choices will add to my stress level and affect my emotional well-being?

Remember, the choices you **make now** have everything to do with your sense of joy and well-being later. Make sure to pick them wisely and carefully because they make up the foundation that your life is built on. Let it be a strong and balanced one that reflects who you are and what you want your life to be!

Stepping Out

We have the ability to stay centered and balanced no matter what is happening around us. Life can throw us all kinds of curve balls. By utilizing the specific strategies in this workbook, not only can we avoid being struck by them, but we can actually hit the balls way out of the field!

In the past, when you felt centered, you were using these strategies. You may not have even realized it! By becoming conscious of what they are and comfortable using them, you will be able to apply these techniques more consistently in your life. The more they are utilized the more in balance you will become!

A fundamental strategy used in living a balanced life is based on our ability to control ourselves when faced with outside events. Instead of trying to control external circumstances or other people, we can choose to think, feel and act in a way that puts our well-being first.

Next time you find yourself getting out of balance, step out of the situation and take an objective look at what is happening. Stop yourself before reacting. Get in touch with what you are thinking and feeling. Assess the situation objectively. Then, think about what you can do to stay in control and in balance. This technique is one of the keys to changing your life. You will be amazed at how powerful it is once you start using it.

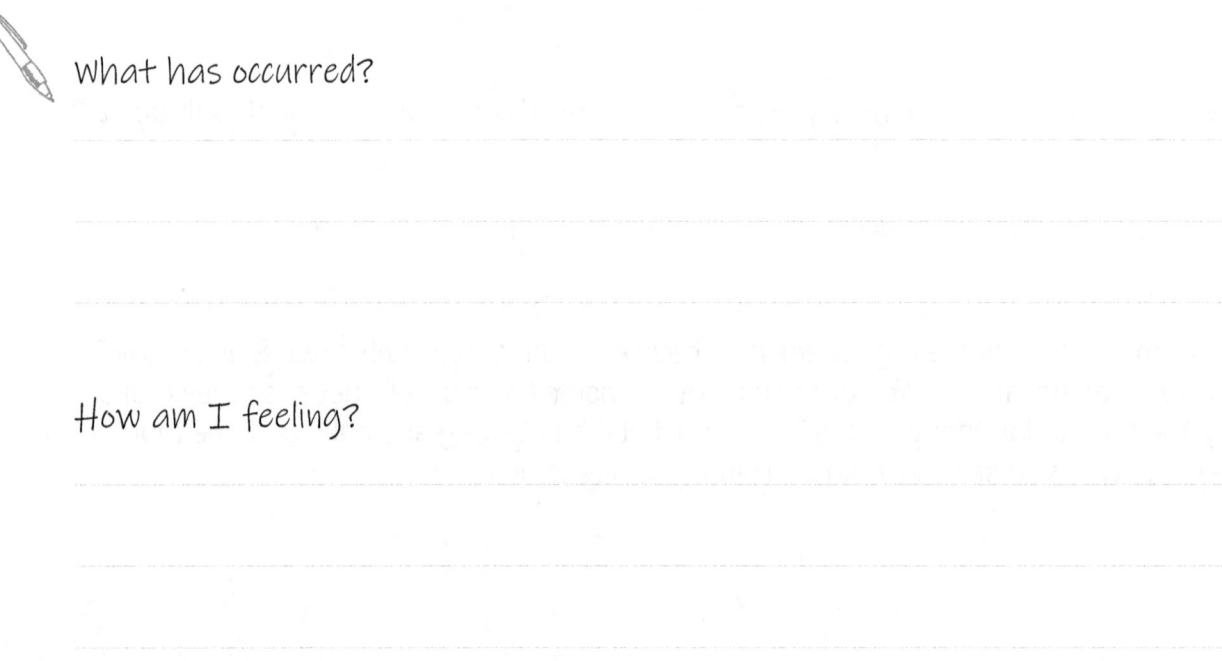

What has occurred?

How am I feeling?

Stepping Out

What is bothering me?

What am I thinking?

What can I do to avoid getting out of balance?

Over-Extending

There are five ways that we all get out of balance. The first one is by over-extending ourselves. We see that there are a certain amount of hours in the day and tend to use most of them for "productive" and goal-oriented activities.

Whether our goals have to do with providing for the needs of our friends and family or are professional or personal, we do not think about how these decisions will impact our inner being. A harsh reality of life for those of us who have so many things that are the "most important" is that there are simply not enough hours in the day to do them all! We must prioritize. We need to make some hard choices if we want more balance in our lives!

To create a life more in balance we need to ask ourselves, "What really is important to me? What do I need to do to accomplish these goals? Which goals will I choose to pursue right now in my life and which will I pursue later?" Answering these questions honestly, and acting on what is discovered are important steps on the path towards Finding The Balance!

What really is important to me right now in my life?

_____

_____

What do I need to do to accomplish these goals?

_____

_____

Realistically, considering the limitations of time and my own limitations in terms of physical, emotional, and mental energy, which goals will I choose to pursue right now?

_____

_____

Which goals will I chose to pursue later?

_____

_____

Prioritizing

The foundation of time management is based on identifying priorities. Create a list of what you want and "need" to do today. Figure out, realistically, how long each activity will take. Next to each item, write down if it is absolutely necessary to do right away, if it can be delegated, or if it can wait.

Re-Evaluating Commitments

In order to regain some balance immediately, it is important to take some time to re-evaluate present commitments. To do this, write out tomorrow's schedule. Now ask yourself this question:

Can all these commitments be accomplished within the time frame I have allocated for them without getting out of balance?

___Yes ___No

If the answer to the question is no, please ask yourself the following question.

Can some of these commitments be put off to a later date, delegated to someone else or eliminated altogether?

___Yes ___No

Based on your answers, re-write your schedule incorporating the knowledge you have gained. When you are finished, ask yourself the same questions in regards to your upcoming weekly, monthly, and yearly commitments.

_____
_____
_____
_____
_____
_____
_____

Re-Evaluating Commitments

Once you get used to making balance a priority, you will start making choices in regard to your time and energy in an entirely different way. You will begin scheduling your life and bringing in new activities, keeping in the forefront of your mind, "How will I feel?" You will allow time to rest, time to be alone, time for fun and time for other activities that will support your desire of Finding the Balance and keeping it.

Following are specific strategies to apply to some situations that tend to throw us all off balance. Through their application, you will gain more control over your happiness and your life. Let's say, for instance, you know that a particular week is going to be unusually packed. Eliminate non-essentials from that week's schedule. Make time in the preceding week and the week that follows for activities that will help you stay in balance. You will certainly feel the difference!

Unexpected things come up in a day and it is important to allow some time in your daily schedule to accommodate them. They do happen, and quite frequently as well. Even so, don't you always seem surprised? If you accept the reality that unplanned things do come up and prepare somewhat for them, you will be much better off. For example, whenever you have to be somewhere at a specific time, make sure to figure in extra time to get there. You never know when you'll run into heavy traffic!

Protect your new plan. If the phone rings and you know that picking it up will throw off your schedule, don't pick it up! Is the stress caused by your rushing afterwards to make up the time worth it? Or let's say that it is the end of the day and you know you have only so much energy and time left. Yet, there is so much you still have to do. Prioritize! Decide what must be done that day, and leave the rest for another day or find another way to get it done. How about when a friend or family member asks you to do something for him or her. Of course you want to say yes. If you simply don't have the time, learn to say no, unless it's an emergency. Often we feel we are being selfish when we do things for ourselves. We may be afraid of what can happen to our relationships if we start setting healthy boundaries. If feeling good inside yourself and having more control of your life is your priority, then you will make these changes. Expect that there might be quite a strong reaction to your new way of being in the world. Remember at those times why you are making these new choices and you will remain firm in your resolve.

Take small steps that you feel are fair and reasonable. Stay true to yourself and know that you are doing this to have more of what you need in life. Keep your eye on how much you can give to others and still stay in balance. When you begin to take better care of yourself, those in your life will learn that if they want you to do something for them, your needs must be taken into consideration.

Re-Evaluating Commitments

When you begin treating yourself with care and respect, others will begin to do so as well. Those who truly love you will be overjoyed at your increased sense of vitality and joy. They will celebrate your new-found sense of freedom and accomplishment. If having more control of your life is your priority, then you will make these changes. By stepping back from the life you have created and by evaluating it from the perspective of inner balance, you will get a clearer picture of what you need to do to create a more balanced life. As challenging as it is to ask the hard questions and to make some difficult decisions, the alternative is for everything to stay the same as it is now. If having a more balanced, fulfilling life is what you desire, your choice is clear.

Now, it is time to write out a new schedule, which will incorporate the strategies that you have acquired. Make some of the tough choices. As your schedule begins to emerge, you will feel your stress being released, and a clearer vision of the life you want...just up ahead! After you have completed this process for tomorrow's schedule, do the same for each day in the month. Congratulations! You are on the road to a more balanced day, month and year!

My New Balanced Schedule

Steps to Fulfillment

Another way we get out of balance is by feeling unfulfilled. Everything on the outside can look good, yet inside of ourselves we are not happy. Usually this is a sign that an important need is not being met. There is something that is essential to our wellbeing that is not being addressed. It is crucial that we take time to think about what that need is. Sometimes we will make the discovery within a short period of time and sometimes it will take much longer.

Once found, taking steps to fulfill it will add a sense of hope and optimism to our lives. We will begin to experience more passion and enthusiasm. Start creating a "space" in your life to dedicate to fulfilling the needs you have identified. Clarify the steps you are going to take and designate time in your daily and weekly schedule for them. If your previous commitments are utilizing all your time and energy, see what changes you can make in the weeks and months ahead to make room for these new goals. Follow this path and you will see new dreams come true.

If you are not in touch with what it is that you need, it is important that you search for the answer. Look within. Learn about yourself by being aware of how you feel in different circumstances and with different people. Notice when you feel good, and notice when you don't. Try new activities. Meet new people. Check in with yourself frequently. You are on a journey of self-discovery. Be patient and it will be a wonderful one.

What important need(s) is not being met?

What steps can I take to meet it?

How can I start filling it in the short term?

What can I plan on doing to be more fulfilled in the near future?

What can I do over the course of the months ahead to fill this need?

The Pieces of My Life

Make a list of the various activities that "make up" your life.

For Example:

Family Rresponsibilities

Work Responsibilities

Time Alone With My Spouse

Fun Time With Family

Social Activities

Community Activities

Hobbies

Vacation Time

Stress Management Activities

My Circle of Life

 **Draw a circle and let this circle represent your life.**

Finding the Balance

My Circle of Life

Now, take out the list you created of the activities that "make up" your life. Designate a section in the circle for each activity on your list. Let each section represent the amount of time spent on that activity. For example, if 25% of your time is spent at work, then the section that represents work should be 25% of the circle. After you have divided your circle into its various sections, take a look at what you have created. What do you see? Do all of the sections of your life fit into the circle? What has your Circle Of Life reflected back to you about the life you have created? Are there empty sections because you have a lot of time that you are not using? Do you need a bigger circle so that everything you are doing will fit into it?

If you need a bigger circle, then an important step you must take is to make certain sections smaller or to actually remove them. It is not possible to be in balance when you have more sections than the circle can contain. Use your Circle of Life to help visualize the life you want. Reflect on what changes are possible and then take actions to make them happen. As difficult as it will be to do, unless you make these adjustments, your life will continue to feel out of balance. Next, draw a circle which reflects these new changes. Once you have gone through this process , you will find that your life is more manageable and in balance.

If you find that your sections do not fill the whole circle, then it is difficult to feel in balance as well. There will usually be a feeling of emptiness, loneliness and/or a lack of fulfillment that comes with an incomplete circle. Think about new activities you can bring in that will make the circle more complete. Then follow the steps outlined above.

If you are looking for a sense of greater fulfillment, then evaluate each section and decide if you would like to devote more or less time to the activity it represents. For example, you might want more time to spend with your friends. Once you have decided what you need to do to make this happen, take the necessary action to bring about those changes. Then adjust the size of that section. Now, look and see if your Circle of Life better reflects the life you want to be living.

Finding the Balance

Getting in Touch

Make a list of your various activities. Indicate next to each one how you feel at the time you are doing them.

_____ I feel _____

_____ I feel _____

_____ I feel _____

Make a list of people you spend time with. Indicate next to each one how you feel when you are with each person individually.

_____ I feel _____

_____ I feel _____

_____ I feel _____

Incorporate the knowledge you have gained into your life. Minimize time spent or eliminate altogether the people and activities you do not enjoy. Start spending more time with those that you do!

Create a list of new activities you will explore.

Finding the Balance

Making Room for New Dreams

Take a look at your weekly and monthly schedule. What changes would you like to make in order to create space to begin manifesting your new dreams.

_____

_____

_____

_____

_____

Write out a "rough draft" of the whole year and for the next five years. Manifesting your dreams begin with visualization, planning, and connecting with the excitement within, with your True Self. Take some time now, to choose the dream you want to manfiest and take the first step right now!

Find your dream and make it happen!

_____

_____

_____

_____

_____

Expectations of Others

Having unrealistic expectations of others is a sure way of losing our sense of centeredness and balance. We all have expectations. We think people should behave in certain ways and we tend to get very upset when they do not act according to what we expect.

How about when we are driving on the freeway and the person behind us is tailgating. If we have the expectation that people should drive safely, we will begin to get annoyed that this person is driving so close to our car. We might try to communicate with the driver by waving our hand in a motion that says, "Back off." Now, maybe that person will accommodate our wishes and maybe he or she won't If the tailgating continues we usually begin to get angry. We have a conversation in our head about what a terrible thing this person is doing. We can't understand how the driver could be so inconsiderate and rude. We might start concentrating on watching the driver in our rear-view mirror, increasing our chance of getting into an accident with the car in front of us.

Our expectation that people should drive safely is realistic, but expecting *this particular ty*pe of driver to do so is not! Our past experiences have shown us that people who tailgate usually continue to do so no matter what we do. To continue interacting with them in any way can only lead to our **getting out of balance**!

This is a truth which holds true in **all** relationships. If we have expectations that are not being met most of the time, then it is likely that these expectations **will** not be met in the future. We need to ask ourself the very important question, "Is what I need from this person so important that I am willing to suffer and be off balance in order to *try* to get him or her to change?" If we are in a relationship with someone who consistently disappoints us, we probably have been waiting quite some time for that person to change...and without too much reward. How much more energy do we want to be putting into the relationship based on how much we have been getting out of it? Is it realistic to expect this person to change? How much are we willing to sacrifice of our own happiness in hopes that the change in the other person will occur? What would it be like if that energy was available to create the life we want and to go after the dreams we *can* obtain?

Expectations of Others

In the situation with the tailgating driver, we allowed this unknown person to get us to some degree out of balance. **Why?** Why should we give away our power? Was that person, or anyone else for that matter, worth losing our sense of joy and happiness? If your answer is *no*, then the way to keep in balance is to ask yourself, "What is more important to me, getting this stranger to do 'the right thing' or keeping my sense of physical, psychological and emotional well-being?" If the answer is the latter, then the next step is to look at your options. What do you need to do to avoid having this negativity around you?

In the case of the tailgating driver, your biggest concern is safety. How do you best insure that? One option is to move over to the other lane. "Oh no," you might say. "That's giving in and allowing the other driver to 'get away' with being rude." Well, maybe it is, but if you step back, look at the bigger picture, and take this action, you have allowed yourself to stay in balance instead of spending valuable minutes or hours interlocked with the negativity of a bad situation. You have also lessened the chances of getting into an accident at the same time.

When we expect something of others that is highly unlikely to happen based on what time has taught us is the reality, we are setting ourselves up to be disappointed. If we expect others to act in the way they usually do instead of in the way we wish they would, we gain more control of our lives. This is another one of the keys to getting and staying in balance. When we accept people as they are, we then have the choice of how we will behave, which in turn leads to our having more control over how we feel. It's not about giving up our values; it's about living life based on its terms, not on our wishes of what we would like it to be. This **shift** will bring you great relief because you can let go of trying to change other people. Instead, you will be able to take control by looking at your options and then deciding what is in your best interest.

Keeping My Power

It is important to become aware of how you give away your power so that you can make the changes necessary to stay connected to it and to your True Self. Here are some questions to ask.

With whom do I most often get disappointed?

What are my expectations of them?

What is it that they do that is so disappointing?

What can I change in my thinking and/or behavior, so that I am no longer as upset and affected by their behaviors?

Is it Personal?

Describe a situation in detail where you felt hurt by someone else.

Is it Personal?

Now, ask yourself these questions:

1. Did I do anything to warrant the unpleasant or hurtful behavior of this person? ___Yes ___No

2. Does the person behave in this manner frequently? ___Yes ___No

3. Does this person behave in this manner with other people? ___Yes ___No

4. Is it possible that the behavior had nothing to do with me or my behavior, but rather had everything to do with that person's personality and internal issues? ___Yes ___No

5. How did I respond to the situation?
_____
_____

6. Did I keep my balance and stay centered? ___Yes ___No

7. Would I do anything different if faced with the same or a similar situation in the future? ___Yes ___No

If yes, what would I do?
_____
_____

Finding the Balance

Should I or Shouldn't I?

Taking responsibility for the quality of our lives is not always easy. Sometimes we have to ask ourselves some tough questions. Think of a person whose behavior you have tried to change. Now ask yourself the following questions.

How successful was I in getting the change I was hoping for?
___Very ___ Somewhat ___ Unsuccessful

Was it worth the effort and heartache up to this point in time? ___Yes ___No

Is it worth risking more heartache? ___Yes ___No

What do I need from this person that I am not getting?
_____
_____

Is the person interested in changing? ___Yes ___No

Does he/she want my help to change? ___Yes ___No

If I make the choice to stop trying to change this person, what changes can I make internally and externally in order to stay centered, balanced and connected with my True Self?
_____
_____

Choosing My Actions

When something happens within ourselves, or outside of ourselves, a chain reaction occurs. First we have thoughts about it, which in turn brings up feelings about it, and ends with our taking some sort of action in relation to it. This process often occurs while we are oblivious that it is taking place.

To take back control over our lives, the first step is to become aware of this internal process and then step in and decide if we want to let it continue to proceed and run its usual course or if we want to intercede on behalf of our desire to stay in balance. In order to stay in balance, choosing our actions is essential. The following process supports our ability to do just that.

First, it is important to think about the various options available and about the consequences that come with each one. Next, it is necessary to consider what we want to create through our actions in the specific situation. Lastly, it is time to make a decision as to what the best course of action will support attaining the desired outcome while connected with our True Self.

Describe a recent situation where you gave away your power because you reacted before taking these steps.

Now revisit the incident applying the steps above. What would the outcome have been?

Finding the Balance

Choosing My Actions

How would utilizing this technique have changed the outcome?

_____

_____

_____

Would you have left with a greater sense of personal power? ___Yes ___No

Did I say what I wanted and in the way I wanted to say it? ___Yes ___No

Did I handle the situation in the best way possible to protect my Center, my self-respect and my balance? ___Yes ___No

What did I learn about myself?

_____

_____

_____

Choosing My Actions

Now, ask the following questions:

What did I learn about the other person?

Did my actions support my staying centered, balanced and connected to my True Self?

What would I do differently?

Cognitive Techniques

Awareness and understanding of our thought process increases our ability to deal effectively with a situation. Here are some cognitive techniques that you can use to help change the way you think and ultimately how you feel.

Self-centering statements – These are phrases you can say to yourself which will help you keep your emotions in balance. By doing so, you can choose which ones you want to keep and which you wish to replace. You must re-evaluate what you were taught as a child in the light of your experiences as an adult.

***SHIFT* Focus** – Choosing to think about something entirely different can prevent your emotions from escalating. Imagine a pleasant event, think of a relaxing scene, sing a song, or count to ten the next time you begin to get upset. Notice how this *SHIFT* in focus causes your emotions to de-escalate.

Empathy – Putting yourself in the "other person's shoes."

Self-Praise – Give yourself credit for the changes you are making. Appreciate yourself for who you truly are.

Remaining Conscious – Remind yourself about the reason you are making this change.

Focusing on the task – Keep in mind why you are controlling your behavior. Detach from the situation if you feel that is your best defense.

Cognitive Techniques

Think of someone with whom you frequently get angry.

Now, write down what that person says that leads to your feeling of anger.

What do you think when he or she says or does it?.

What cognitive techniques can you utilize in the future that will enable you to avoid getting off balance?

If you replace your original thoughts with these new thoughts, how will it affect your reaction?

Applying these steps to challenging situations as they occur to change the quality of your inner and outer world. Develop this skill and you will transform your life!

Taking Action

To change our lives, we must take action. We are able to choose to change our thoughts, to replace critical and judgmental thoughts about ourselves with words of understanding and compassion. We get to choose who we have in our lives. The people we surround ourselves with impacts the quality of our lives. Take some time now to consider the changes you would like to make in the way you thing and act with...

strangers you come in contact with throughout the course of a day

casual acquaintances

family members

specific friends

Expectations of Myself

The principles that apply to unrealistic expectations of others also apply to unrealistic expectations of ourselves. If there is something that we want to create, it is essential to look at ourselves honestly to gain greater understanding. We can look at what supported us in accomplishing what we set out to do as well as what did not. By doing so, we can have a more realistic view of how we are in the world right now.

This is extremely freeing and empowering. When we base our actions on this knowledge and learn from the past, we are able to create change based on knowing ourselves and what has supported change in the past and what has not. this approach allows for to become open to new ways of being in the world that support what we want to create as we move forward in our lives.

Does that mean we shouldn't try to change things we wish to improve about ourselves? No! If there is something that we want to accomplish we should continue to put in the effort, even if we haven't succeeded in the past. Should we be hard on ourselves and put ourselves down if we don't accomplish it? Being harsh and critical of ourselves does not help us reach our goal. It actually makes us less likely to achieve it in the future. Negative self-talk only serves to undermine our confidence, which in turn affects our ability to succeed.

It is more realistic to expect that what we are choosing to accomplish will be challenging. Going into it with this knowledge then allows us to look for new options. Being realistic gives us a better chance of reaching our goal.

Finding the Balance

Supporting Myself

What is one area in my life where I would like to create change?

What thoughts will support creating this change and staying connected with my True Self?

What have a learned from the past that I can utilize to manifesting my desire?

Are there new ways I can approach an old challenge that are worth trying?
___ Yes ___ No

Which approach might increase the likelihood of a positive outcome?

Choosing Happiness

Happiness is a choice. Regardless of what happens around us, we can choose to be happy. Even when we experience a tremendous loss or number of losses, we can survive. In time, it is even possible to be happy again.

The key to happiness lies within each of us. When tragedies occur we have all the reasons to validate our unhappiness. We are justified in our true misery. But we must ask ourselves, "Is this how I want to feel for the rest of my life? Do I want to always be unhappy, angry, and depressed?" If your answer is no, then there is a way to feel joy again.

It does take a while because the pain of the loss is so great. Until the pain lessens, the first step of the process is to make it through and to survive the pain. Eventually we are able to go through longer and longer periods of time without suffering as much. That is when we regain some of our energy. We can begin to engage with the world anew.

The way to feel happiness again is by focusing our mind away from how awful things seem and thoughts of "How can I go on without the person I love? How can I go on without that which I have lost? What will I do with my life now that I am unable to go after my dream?" Rather, we need to replace these thoughts with others. A powerful tool is to think about all of our blessings. We need to appreciate all that we have instead of focusing on what we have lost. Even though life as we have known it may have changed in many ways, a world of possibilities is just around the corner.

As time continues to march on, as it always does, we slowly are able to build a new life for ourselves. If it includes those who love and support us, and activities old and new that are fulfilling, happiness can be attained. The loss will always be there, but a lot of new people and passions will be there as well. It takes patience, courage and strength to survive loss and to embrace life once again. Know that you deserve to be happy. Put one step ahead of the last, and in time you will feel your passion return and a new-found sense of who you are along with it.

Finding the Balance

Surviving Loss

If you have experienced a terrible loss, whether it is the loss of a love one, the loss of your family unit, loss of your health or the ability to go after a dream, and you want to have more joy in you life, it is important to ask these questions.

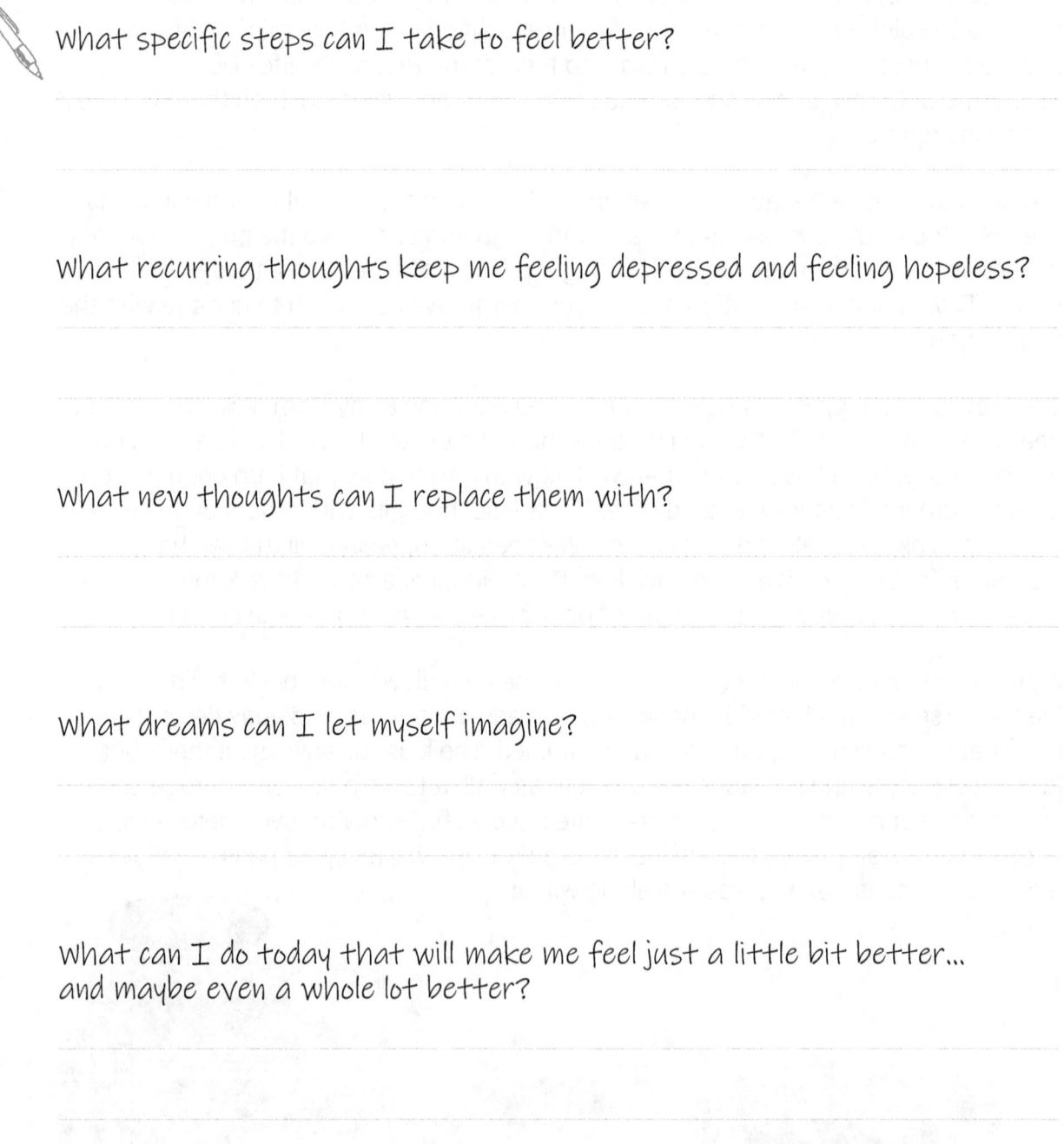

What specific steps can I take to feel better?

What recurring thoughts keep me feeling depressed and feeling hopeless?

What new thoughts can I replace them with?

What dreams can I let myself imagine?

What can I do today that will make me feel just a little bit better... and maybe even a whole lot better?

Staying In Balance

My Well-Being, My Priority

Once you have integrated these strategies into your life and have learned to utilize some of the tools as well, how do you stay in balance? The first and most important action to take is to **Protect Your Center**. To do so requires that your put your well-being, your balance, as your priority. You need to be your own top priority in your life. That doesn't mean that you will stop being a giving and loving person. It means that you will be giving and loving to yourself. Shouldn't you be as important as those you give to? Don't you deserve to treat yourself as well as you treat others? By applying the new skills you have learned consistently throughout your day, you can and will feel better with each new day. Your sense of joy and inner strength will grow. Is it possible to be happy and fulfilled most of the time? *Yes!* The answer is Yes!

The way to make this happen is to protect your Center. Staying conscious of your inner state of calm and peace and being aware of anything that may enter in that is disruptive, allows you to take the actions necessary to stay connected with your True Self, centered and in balance. Imagine your Center as a clear, still lake. It is calm and serene. When something enters into this space, it causes a ripple or sometimes even a splash! First, the cause of this disruption needs to be identified, and then your new knowledge and tools need to be utilized until this lake is still again. Whether the calm was shaken by a reaction to an external or internal source, you *can* calm your inner lake, your Center. Staying in balance is about being aware of your Center and keeping it in a state of serenity and balance.

Finding the Balance

Journal Writing

Keeping an on-going journal of people, thoughts, emotions and situations that disrupt the "still of our lake" is helpful in this process. We can, then, utilize this knowledge to gain greater insights, understanding and life skills to support our living in balance. Staying conscious and applying our gained wisdom throughout our life, will lead to greater balance and happinessFinding the Balance is a lifelong process. Each time you get out of balance and utilize the skills you have acquired, you are taking the steps in creating the happiness you deserve.

Finding the Balance

Protecting My Center

In order to create more happiness in your life, it is extremely helpful to identify recurring situations in which you tend to get out of balance. By becoming aware of when, how, and with whom they occur, you can take steps to protect your Center. Whether you choose to avoid putting yourself in these situations, or whether you choose to utilize your new skills and deal with them, you are in control! Ask yourself the following questions and see what insights you gain!

What is a recurring situation in which I tend to get out of balance?

_____
_____
_____
_____

Describe the situation in detail.

_____
_____
_____
_____

Protecting My Center

When was the last time it occurred?

Was the cause internal or external?

How did I deal with it?

Utilizing my new knowledge, what can I do when it happens again to stay in balance?

Getting it on Paper

Sometimes we get so overwhelmed with everything we need to do that it helps to write it down. By getting our thoughts out of our head and onto a piece of paper, we are able to gain a sense of control and relief!

Make a list of all the errands that you need to do right now. Choose which ones you will do today and which you will do later. You will find that many of them can be scheduled in throughout the week or weeks ahead. Now...take a deep breath!!!

Simplifying My Life

There are specific actions we can take that will lessen the stress in our day-to-day lives. First, it is necessary to identify the stressors so that we can, then, organize our lives in a way to gain greater control. A helpful technique is to put the things we use on a daily basis in the same place every time after using them. For instance, we can place the remote control and our keys in designated spots so that when we need them we know where to find them. This simple act can save a tremendous amount of time and stress!

Another way to simplify our lives is by buying extra quantities of items that we frequently use and often run out of. How often have we had to rush out to the store at less than opportune times, because we didn't have something that we really needed right then and there. Doing things in advance can also help make our lives more manageable. Preparing soup, and other meals and then freezing them is a perfect example. By planning ahead, we are taking control of the quality of our life.

When we put our balance as a priority, new ideas and options open up that we had never considered before. It is this change in perspective that give us the ability to transform our lives one step at a time.

Think of ways that you can organize your life so that you can maintain your balance with less daily effort.

Conflict Resolution

In order to stay in balance, it is necessary to know how to deal with conflict when it arises. To be successful, we must have strong inner self-control and the ability to utilize our emotional intelligence. We practice inner self-control when we don't immediately react to an external occurrence. It is important to be able to step back from the situation long enough to grasp a more complete picture of what is going on.

This is an essential skill to have if we want to be successful in resolving conflicts and having healthy relationships. Allowing ourselves time to listen to our intuition is extremely valuable as well. During a conflict, it is imperative that we are aware of what is happening on many different levels. Using our emotional intelligence allows us to gain a deeper understanding of the other person and of the situation.

Often external conflict is **only a reflection** of what the real problem is. We must look for a more complete perspective concerning what is going on. At times, what a person really thinks and feels is different from what his or her words are communicating. The person may not even be aware of his or her true feelings.

This can make communication between two people extremely challenging, confusing, and difficult. At moments like this, it is invaluable to rely on our emotional intelligence and to listen on many different levels to "hear" what **really** is being said.

For example, if your sixteen year old teenage daughter seems to be opposing you at every turn, it may appear on the outside that all she cares about is doing what she wants. If you look deeper, you may find there is an underlying cause for her behavior. Perhaps she is feeling unloved, or thinks she has disappointed you.

By understanding what is below the surface, you will have the ability to approach the conflict from a different angle. You will respond differently than you would have without your newly gained insight. Your new perspective will in turn open up a whole new set of options in how to deal with the conflict and the relationship.

Conflict Resolution

When a conflict begins, it helps to stop, step out of the situation and try to see it from the other person's point of view. A key to conflict resolution is the ability to empathize with the other person. When we are empathetic, the other person in the conflict can sense it. Sincere empathy has the effect of changing the whole tone of the conflict. Treating the other person with respect is extremely important as well. When others feel valued they respond to us in a completely different manner. We need to value ourselves too. Making the choice to conduct ourselves in a way that we can be proud of is being true to our Center. As difficult as it may be, name-calling and swearing should be avoided. "Hitting below the belt" must be eliminated from confrontations altogether. When we put the other person down or bring up something he or she is very sensitive about, we do irreparable damage to the relationship.

When in the midst of a conflict, remember what your ultimate goals are. By taking control of your actions, you will be on the road to resolving the conflict at hand and insuring more productive and positive interactions in the future.

Emotional Intelligence

Describe a recent conflict.

Where did it occur and with whom?

How did you react?

What did you say or do?

Emotional Intelligence

Was your reaction based on what the other person said, or on what your emotional intelligence was telling you was the deeper cause of the conflict?

_____

_____

_____

_____

Did you stay in balance? ___ Yes ___ No

If you didn't, what did you learn from the experience? What could you do differently in the future?

_____

_____

_____

_____

_____

Problem-Solving

Often we are faced with problems that seem insurmountable. Applying these six steps to the situation is helpful in gaining control and a sense of relief.

Step 1: Identify the true problem using both your cognitive and emotional intelligence.

Step 2: Create a list of possible solutions to the problem.

Step 3: Identify the probable outcome of each of the possible solutions.

Step 4: Choose the solution that takes into consideration your needs and desires.

Step 5: Develop a plan of action. How will you go about solving the problem using the solution you have decided on.

Step 6: Implement the chosen plan.

What problem are you currently facing?

_____

_____

_____

_____

_____

Now go through each step and apply it to that problem. By using the process on a regular basis, you will find that you will feel more in control of your life. Be patient with yourself. You are on your way to transforming your life...one step at a time!

On-Going Challenges

Sometimes we are in situations at home and at work where we are dealing with people who do not treat us with the respect and consideration we deserve. Remember, we always have the choice to no longer put ourselves in these situations. We must weigh our various interests and resources and then make a decision. Whether we stay in the situation or not, we now have the tools to take better care of ourselves and our inner well-being. Remember, it is the way we deal with life's challenges that creates the quality of our lives.

Identify a challenging situation. Do I choose to stay in it? Why, or why not?

On-Going Challenges

 If I choose to leave, what steps will I take and when?

If I choose to stay, what steps will I take to protect myself and maintain my Center to the best of my ability in this situation.

How long will I stay?

What is my exit plan?

Sometimes you might choose to stay in such an environment because you are choosing "short term pain for long term gain." Or maybe you are taking steps to get out of it, but it will take some time before you can leave.

It is essential that, during this period, you take especially good care of yourself. Schedule in frequent, short intervals when you can get away. Involve yourself in activities that will replenish your depleted resources and which will help you get re-centered. These activities might include taking a walk alone or with a friend, going into your car and listening to a great CD, or running over to Starbucks and getting your favorite *non-caffeinated* drink!

In addition, schedule elements into your daily, monthly, yearly calendar that supports your happiness. Allow time to prepare for your exit plan. This is the way to create the more balanced life you are looking to achieve.

Inner Growth

Because of your effort and perseverance you have acquired new tools and skills that can now be applied to the challenges life presents. This new knowledge and awareness can significantly enhance the quality of your life. Take a look now at your responses to the exercise "The Process of Becoming Aware" on page 12. Ask yourself how you would handle those situations if they were to occur now. Times when I...

was over-extended

was affected by other people's behavior

felt unfulfilled

was disappointed with others

was disappointed in myself

was devastated because something terrible happened

Diagramming My Support

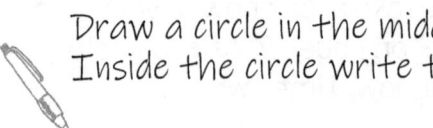 Draw a circle in the middle of the page. Inside the circle write the word "me."

Now look at the list of people and groups who are a in your life. Place these names inside and outside the circle depending on the degree of support you get from them. Some names might be placed on the rim of the circle, others might be next to the edges of the sheet of paper. Seeing your personal support in this format will help you become more aware of the people in your life whom you can turn to when in need. When you look at the diagram, do you feel that you have enough support? If you would like more, what can you do to bring more into your life?

Stress Management

At the first signs of getting out of balance our body gets tense. Throughout the course of the day, most of us are involved in a variety of situations in which we get stressed out. Following are some techniques that are useful in de-stressing at the moments we become aware of our stress. Others can be integrated into our life on a regular basis. What can you add to the list?

Deep breathing

Relaxation techniques

Exercising

Nutritious meals

Positive self-talk

Fun activities with others

Fun activities alone

Sleeping

Music

Dancing

Laughing

Reading

Getting a massage

Yoga

Smelling the roses

De-Stressing Techniques

It is important to take care of ourselves so that we are better equipped to deal with life's stressors. By doing so, we will enjoy our lives more fully.

Make a list of de-stressing techniques that you will use in the future when you know that you will be going into a stressful situation or time period.

_____

_____

_____

_____

_____

Do some techniques work better for you at certain times than at others?
___Yes ___ No

Which can you incorporate into your daily life and which into your weekly, monthly, and yearly calendar?

_____

_____

_____

_____

_____

A Balanced Lifestyle

To have a balanced lifesytle, we will want to create a balance between work, responsbiilities, fun and relaxation. Enjoying a healthy diet, regular exercise, adequate sleep, and a balance of hobbies and pleasurable activities provides a solid foundation of resources to manage stress and enables us to have a happier and healthier life. Learning to arrange our time so we are not stressed from trying to do too much is an important part as well.

Talking to supportive friends, relatives, colleagues and professionals can help reinforce the positive changes we are making and can encourage us in our new efforts. Spending time with those we care about and who care about us helps us "weather the storm" and enjoy the good times too! Involvement in religious and community activities is a way of giving to others and to ourselves. The sense of fulfillment can be immense.

Having a positive philosophy can make all the difference in how we feel about our lives. In the place of worrying about the circumstance and people we cannot control, we can put our focus on what we can. Counting our blessings and never taking them for granted allows us to feel gratitude for the wonderful gifts we have. When we look at what we have instead of what we don't have, we have taken another important step toward the happiness and joy we are seeking. Never forget that the greatest gift you have...is yourself! Always dream and know that you have the power to go after those dreams and change your reality.

Living From Your Center

Connected to My True Self

You have now completed the workbook Finding The Balance: *A Guide To Sane Living.* By stepping back and looking at life from a new perspective, you have gained a greater awareness of yourself and a deeper understanding of the world of which you are a part.

Now it is time to transform your life! Have you made the decision to live from your Center and make it a priority? Are you determined to live a happier and more balanced life? The choice is yours to make.

In the days, weeks, and months to come, apply the new tools, strategies and skills that you have worked so diligently to acquire towards these goals. Let the feelings of joy and optimism that you begin every morning with be the same ones you have at the end of every wonderful day. The next step of your journey is just up ahead. Let it be one filled with passion and fulfillment. Trust in yourself and in your ability to **Find The Balance**, and truly know that you do have the power to create the life of your dreams! Now, go make it happen!.

About The Author

Bonnie Barness, M.A.,LISAC, is from Beverly Hills, California and is a graduate of U.C.L.A. She currently resides in Scottsdale, Arizona, where she maintains a private practice and *SHIFT* Life Coaching.

As a licensed psychotherapist, mediator, behavioral consultant and anger management specialist, Ms. Barness works with individuals, couples, families, organizations, schools, and companies to resolve conflict, enhance performance and reach their goals. In her advice column "Ask Bonnie," she gives concrete solutions to challenges we all face. In addition, Ms Barness appears on On radio, television and social media, and writes for a variety of newspapers.

Through her books, workbooks, workshops, teleseminars and weekend reatreats, Ms. Barness supports individuals of all ages make dreams into reality. She also offers *SHIFT* Actualization®. She also offers Training programs to professionals, businesses, clinics, and organizations who want to support others in Experiencing the *SHIFT* in their personal lives and within the workplace. For more information, please go to BonnieBarness.com. If you are interested in private sessions, *SHIFT* AP Executive Coaching, offering SHIFT Actualization® seminars, workshop, retreats or Trainings or would like to sign-up to become a *SHIFT* AP Facilitator or Practitioner, please email BonnieBarness@yahoo.com.

Copyright © 2022
by Bonnie Barness
All Rights Reserved.
All images ©2005 pamelabreece.com
Graphic Design by Amy Taylor
Copy-editing by Morton Tuchin

www.ingramcontent.com/pod-product-compliance
Lightning Source LLC
Chambersburg PA
CBHW060530010526
44110CB00052B/2552